BRILLIANT WOMEN

HEROIC LEADERS AND ACTIVISTS

Written by Georgia Amson-Bradshaw
Illustrated by Rita Petruccioli

WAYLAND
www.waylandbooks.co.uk

CONTENTS

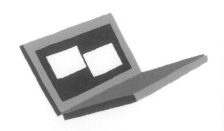

HEROIC LEADERS AND ACTIVISTS

Do you have a favourite superhero? A character who fights evil, battles the bad guys and stands up for the weak against the strong? From Hercules to Wonder Woman, stories of brave heroes who risk life and limb to defeat the forces of darkness have been told and enjoyed for thousands of years.

But although tales of warriors and strong men and women fighting monsters and criminals are thrilling, the real-life challenges faced by real-life heroines are much harder. The incredible, fearless women in this book have fought battles for many years of their lives, and they haven't always been celebrated for it.

Social activists who challenge injustice have to fight their own societies. They need to have the wisdom, strength and heart to see that the situation they are living in is unfair, even when many of the people around them are telling them they are wrong.

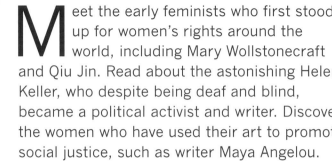

M eet the early feminists who first stood up for women's rights around the world, including Mary Wollstonecraft and Qiu Jin. Read about the astonishing Helen Keller, who despite being deaf and blind, became a political activist and writer. Discover the women who have used their art to promote social justice, such as writer Maya Angelou.

These inspiring activists for peace, human rights and the environment have all, in their own ways, made their mark on history.

If you feel deeply about a particular cause, or if you can see a way in which the world could be changed for the better, you'll find ideas in this book for how to make a difference. There are suggestions for how to raise awareness for your favourite cause, raise money for charity and contact your elected politicians to make your voice heard!

Anyone can make a difference. Even you. Especially you. So get ready to be inspired by these brilliant, real-life superheroes!

MARY WOLLSTONECRAFT

A trailblazing writer and thinker, Mary Wollstonecraft argued for women's rights and education at a time when women were treated as men's property.

FEMINIST PHILOSOPHER

Mary Wollstonecraft wrote about big ideas such as morality, what an ideal society should be like, and equality between men and women.

LIVED:	*27 April 1759 – 10 September 1797*
BORN IN:	London (UK)
WORKED IN:	London (UK)

As a girl, Mary was treated unfairly from the day she was born. Her parents gave her brother Edward much more attention. During the time that Mary was born, boy children were celebrated, whereas girl children were considered a financial burden. Daughters were not able to carry on the family name once they married, and everything they owned became the property of their new husband. Women were also expected to obey their husbands entirely, and while men could divorce their wives for having an affair, women could not get a divorce from their husband for the same reason.

Mary left home when she was 19, and worked as a teacher and then a governess. She was very frustrated by the lack of job opportunities for women, and in 1787 she decided to take a radical step – trying to earn her living by becoming an author. This was not at all normal for women at the time, and Mary told her sister she would be 'the first of a new genus'.

She worked for a publisher in London, translating political and philosophical pamphlets. It was during this time that she met political activists and philosophers such as Thomas Paine. Thomas Paine wrote a book called *Rights of Man,* which set out the rights that a citizen should have in their country. During the 18th century, countries such as France and the USA were experiencing a lot of political change, and the ideas in *Rights of Man* were very influential.

I do not wish women to have power over men; but over themselves.

Mary wrote her most famous pamphlet, *A Vindication of the Rights of Woman*, in 1792. In it, she argued that women should not be considered 'ornaments' or the property of men, but that they should be treated as human beings with the same basic rights. She argued that, as women were responsible for teaching and raising children, it was for the good of everyone that women be educated properly. At the time, many people assumed that women could not think rationally like men.

When Mary published her pamphlet, it was initially well-received, but later people dismissed her work because of 'scandalous' things she had done (which included having a daughter with a man she wasn't married to). Nowadays, her work is considered incredibly important, as she was one of the earliest feminist writers.

WRITE A PAMPHLET LIKE MARY

During the 18th century, many political thinkers and philosophers wrote pamphlets that set out their opinions on how society ought to be. Write your own political pamphlet! Think about what you believe to be unfair or wrong about the world at the moment. Perhaps you think children shouldn't be forced by their parents to go to school? Or do you think people shouldn't eat animals? Decide what would be different in your perfect world, and write your arguments down on a piece of paper. Give it to your friends and family to read.

HARRIET TUBMAN

Born a slave, the tireless and brave Harriet Tubman escaped from her masters and then risked her life over and over again to help other slaves reach freedom.

ABOLITIONIST

Harriet was part of the abolition movement, which was the campaign to end slavery in the USA and Europe. Campaigners and activists spoke out against slavery, and helped slaves escape.

LIVED:	c. 1820 – 10 March 1913
BORN IN:	Dorchester County, Maryland (USA)
WORKED IN:	Pennsylvania and Maryland (USA)

Harriet Tubman was born in Maryland, USA. Her mum was called Harriet, too, and her dad was called Benjamin. They were both slaves, and this meant Harriet was a slave too. Her master treated her very cruelly, and when she was only five years old she was given the job of looking after a baby. When she couldn't stop the baby from crying, she was whipped.

Harriet's master died when she was 27 years old. She decided it would be better to try and run away, rather than be sold again. She knew that if she could get to the neighbouring state of Pennsylvania, where slavery was illegal, she would be free. Harriet headed north using the Underground Railroad. This wasn't an actual railway, but a network of slaves, freed slaves, and white abolitionists who would help runaway slaves escape by hiding them in their houses, or transporting them to a new safe house.

Harriet travelled at night to avoid detection. When she crossed over into Pennsylvania, she had to check her hands to see if she was the same person! She later said, 'there was such a glory over everything ... I felt like I was in heaven.' She lived in Pennsylvania and worked odd jobs to earn money, but she was not content with just her own freedom. She wanted to help others to be free.

Over the next 11 years, Harriet returned to Maryland again and again, to guide first her family, and then other slaves, to freedom. She made about 13 expeditions, and guided around 70 slaves to freedom, as well as providing directions to another 50 or 60. During her rescue missions she would travel at night, or disguise herself as a slave on an errand by carrying a chicken.

When the American Civil War (1861–1865) began between the Unionists (made up of northern US states where slavery was illegal) and the Confederates (made up of southern US states where slavery was legal), Harriet worked as a nurse and a spy for the Union forces. Despite her service during and after the war, she did not receive a salary from the US government and spent her whole life living in poverty.

CAMPAIGN AGAINST SLAVERY LIKE HARRIET

Did you know there are more people enslaved around the world today than there were when Harriet was alive? Although slavery is illegal worldwide, in many places the law is not enforced. As a result, up to 30 million people, many of whom are women and children, are slaves right now. Many famous abolitionists during Harriet's day were preachers, who stood up and made speeches against slavery. Why don't you research, write and perform your own speech about modern-day slavery to your family and friends? You can find out about which organisations are working to combat it, and tell your friends and family how they can help.

EGLANTYNE JEBB

Although she came from a well-off background, Eglantyne was outraged by the suffering of the poor, particularly children.

HUMANITARIAN

Eglantyne felt her calling in life was to save human lives and reduce human suffering.

LIVED:	25 August 1876 – 17 December 1928
BORN IN:	Ellesmere (UK)
WORKED IN:	UK and Switzerland

Eglantyne had a happy childhood. She was born into a well-off family in England with a big house. She loved horse riding, and spent her summers climbing trees, swimming and boating on the lake. In the winter she would go ice skating. She was very imaginative, and loved reading, writing and telling stories. She would tell stories to her younger brothers and sisters about heroes and monsters, magicians and witches.

Although Eglantyne's family wealth meant she didn't have to work, she was determined to do something useful. After graduating from university she started working as a primary school teacher. While she was training to be a teacher in East London she saw many children in poverty, who were ill and weak due to lack of food. Later, while doing charity work in Cambridge, she realised that poverty in England was a serious and widespread problem.

During and after the First World War (1914–1918), Great Britain, France and Russia blockaded Germany and its allies. This meant they stopped food and other goods being imported into the countries, in order to weaken them and bring about the end of the war. However, food shortages in Germany after the First World War meant many children were starving.

Eglantyne was appalled that British actions were causing children to die. She gave out leaflets in Trafalgar Square in London showing two starving German children, with the caption 'Our blockade has caused this!'. She was arrested and tried for her protest, but the prosecutor was so impressed with her actions that he paid her fine himself!

You're fined ... but I'm paying!

Eglantyne soon realised that protest alone wouldn't change the situation. Real aid was desperately needed, so with some help from her sister, Dorothy Buxton, she set up the charity Save the Children, which raised money from the British public and organised food to be distributed to starving children across Europe. In Russia alone in 1921 and 1922, Save the Children food aid helped to keep 300,000 children and 350,000 adults alive.

But Eglantyne also realised that no matter how generous, charity was not enough either. To make a lasting change, children's rights needed to be defended by the law. She drafted a document, the 'Declaration of the Rights of the Child', which was adopted by the international organisation, the League of Nations, in 1924. This document also became the basis of current international law on children's rights, which is outlined in the United Nations Convention on the Rights of the Child.

RAISE FUNDS FOR SAVE THE CHILDREN LIKE EGLANTYNE

Save the Children is still a large and successful international organisation that fights for children's rights and provides relief to children suffering from disasters around the world. Save the Children have lots of ideas for ways you can help raise money to support the work that they do on their website, from hosting den-building parties to sponsored walks or bike rides. Take a look and see which ideas appeal to you, and organise a fundraising event of your own. There are lots of other charities that help children. See if you can find one in your local area that needs support.

HELEN KELLER

Despite losing her sight and hearing as a baby, Helen Keller's incredible intelligence and determination enabled her to become a world-famous author and political activist.

ADVOCATE FOR THE BLIND

An advocate argues for the rights of a particular person or group. Helen Keller travelled and advocated for improvements in the conditions of blind peoples' lives.

LIVED:	27 June 1880 – 1 June 1968
BORN IN:	Tuscumbia, Alabama (USA)
WORKED IN:	USA and worldwide

A healthy, happy baby named Helen was born into a well-off family in Alabama in the summer of 1880. But, when she was only 19 months old, Helen lost her sight and hearing after a mysterious illness. As she got older, being unable to communicate properly made Helen a bad-tempered, naughty child.

Helen's parents arranged for her to have a teacher, Anne Sullivan, who came to live with them. Anne arrived in 1897 and began teaching Helen using finger spelling. She would teach Helen words by spelling them out on the palm of Helen's hand. For example, Anne spelled D-O-L-L, then passed Helen her doll. Helen didn't understand at first, and became very frustrated. Then, about one month after Anne began using finger spelling, Anne traced the letters W, A, T, E, R on Helen's hand, while holding her hand to water. Helen suddenly understood! She was so excited that she learned the hand spelling for 30 different objects in one day.

With Anne to help her, Helen went to school in 1888. She was a very bright student, and she learned several methods of communication, including lip-reading by touch (where she would place her fingers against the mouth of the speaking person), braille (a system of written letters that use raised dots on paper that can be felt by the fingertips), typing, and even speech!

Helen learned to speak by feeling the vibrations and lip-movements of her teachers, and copying them. Although her speech was not perfect, it was an incredible achievement. She went to university, studying at Radcliffe College. She was accompanied by Anne who translated her texts and lectures for her. Helen was the first deaf-blind person ever to graduate from university. It was while she was a student that Helen wrote her first book, *The Story of My Life*.

After graduating Helen became a writer, political activist and advocate. She gave many speeches as well as writing books and essays on various topics, including religion, disabled people's rights and politics. She was appointed to a role within the American Foundation of Overseas Blind, and she travelled to over 40 different countries arguing in favour of education, treatment and rights for the blind.

COMMUNICATE LIKE HELEN

Sighted and hearing people can help blind and deaf people by learning ways to communicate with them. Using the braille alphabet below, have a go at writing a letter using braille. Get a piece of paper, a piece of cardboard and a biro. Put the paper on top of the cardboard, and press the biro down to make raised bumps on the reverse side of the paper. But wait! The braille is read on the reverse side of the paper. This means you need to write it as though it is a mirror image of what you want to end up with, so start on the right-hand side of your paper and move left, and flip the dot patterns of the letters too. Keep practising until you figure it out!

A	B	C	D	E	F	G	H	I
J	K	L	M	N	O	P	Q	R
S	T	U	V	W	X	Y	Z	

FAITH BANDLER

Faith's own experiences of injustice, as well the suffering of her father, propelled her to fight for equality in a deeply unfair society.

INDIGENOUS RIGHTS CAMPAIGNER

Faith organised petitions and meetings to get Australian law changed to recognise equal rights for indigenous people.

LIVED: 27 September 1918 – 13 February 2015

BORN IN: Tumbulgum, New South Wales (Australia)

WORKED IN: Australia

Faith was one of eight children. Her mum, Ida, had Scottish and Indian heritage. Her dad, Wacvie Mussingkon (who later changed his name to Peter Mussing) was an indigenous South Sea Islander. For much of his life, Wacvie had worked as a slave labourer on Australian sugar plantations, after being 'blackbirded' from the small South Sea nation of Vanuatu when he was 13 years old. 'Blackbirding' was the term for capturing and kidnapping indigenous people, taking them away on boats and forcing them to work as cheap or unpaid labourers. This was a common method of finding workers for the sugar industry in Australia in the 19th century.

Are you kidding me?

After 20 years on the plantations, Wacvie escaped, but his life story inspired Faith in her activism. Faith was a very good student at school, but the Great Depression in the 1930s stopped her studies. She worked various jobs, including on farms, where she was paid less than the white workers, as were the Aboriginal Australians and other indigenous people from the region.

Indigenous people were treated very badly by the Australian government, and weren't even considered worthy of counting when the government did a census. Indigenous people were forced to live in designated areas, and the children of indigenous families were often forcibly removed from their parents.

After working as a seamstress and on fruit farms, Faith became a full-time activist in 1956, campaigning for indigenous people's rights. She led a campaign to change the Constitution of Australia to remove the discrimination against indigenous people, organising several huge petitions and hundreds of large public meetings. Eventually, in 1967 her campaign was successful. A key referendum was held that changed the law in Australia so that indigenous people were included in the census as well, making it possible for the government to create laws that would help the indigenous population.

After her great success with the campaign that led to the 1967 referendum, Faith started to focus her energy on the plight of her own people, the descendants of South Sea Islanders who were still not eligible for certain benefits in education, health and housing. In 1976 she made an emotional journey to the South Sea island of Ambrym in Vanuatu, where her father was kidnapped so many years before.

CREATE POLITICAL CHANGE LIKE FAITH

Although children can't vote in referendums or elections, there are no age limits on learning about politics and campaigning during referendums or at election time! Why not look online to read up on the policies of the different political parties, and decide which ones sound the best to you. You might particularly want to look at what policies they have about children and young people. How would the ideas they put forward affect you? You can also write to your local politician to ask for their support on a campaign that you feel strongly about.

SOPHIE SCHOLL

Sophie's powerful sense of right and wrong led the young student to stand up against the Nazi regime in Germany, and ultimately to give her life for her beliefs.

PACIFIST

Being a pacifist means believing in non-violence. Sophie rejected the brutality of the Nazis, and encouraged others to resist them using peaceful means.

LIVED:	9 May 1921 – 22 February 1943
BORN IN:	Forchtenberg (Germany)
WORKED IN:	Munich (Germany)

Sophie was one of six children. Her dad, Robert, was the mayor of the small town of Forchtenberg where the family lived. Sophie's strong sense of justice was apparent from an early age. At school, the best pupils had to sit on the front row. On her younger sister Elizabeth's birthday, Elizabeth was moved by the teacher from the front row to the second row. Sophie was so angry at the unfairness of her sister being moved off the front row on her birthday, that she escorted her sister back to the front row and told the teacher 'It's Elizabeth's birthday, so I'm moving her back!'

Not today, teacher!

Sophie was eleven when the Nazis, led by Adolf Hitler, came to power in 1933. At first she joined the League of German Maidens, which was the girls' wing of the Nazi youth movement, but as she learned more about Nazi ideology, she realised how wrong the ideas of the Nazi Party were.

The Nazis believed that white people were superior, that disabled people were a burden, and that any political opposition was treason. Activities like making jokes about the Nazis or forming a youth group that wasn't part of the Hitler Youth was made illegal. Jewish people were seen as 'subhuman', and a danger to society. In 1939 Nazi-led Germany invaded Poland, which started the Second World War (1939–1945).

After finishing school, Sophie began to work as a nursery teacher, and then started studying at the University of Munich in 1942 where her brother Hans was also a student. At university, Sophie and Hans and a group of friends who called themselves the 'White Rose' began to create pamphlets that called on people to resist the Nazis. The pamphlets argued that the Nazi regime was criminal and oppressive, and they condemned the mass-murder of Jewish people that the Nazi government was conducting. They urged people to take up non-violent resistance, through protest and political non-cooperation.

After dropping some leaflets, Sophie and Hans were spotted and reported to the secret police. A draft of a leaflet written by another member, Christoph Probst, was found in Hans' apartment. The three of them were put on trial and sentenced to death. They were executed by guillotine on 22 February, 1943. The incredible bravery of Sophie and all of the members of the White Rose group has since inspired millions of people. In Germany, they have become a symbol of resistance against tyranny, and many monuments have been erected in their honour.

PROTEST LIKE SOPHIE

Non-violent resistance has been an important technique for social activists for a long time, and continues to be used to make political change today. Key methods include going on demonstrations or protest marches. Join a demonstration for an issue that you care about – or if you can't find one, why not organise one yourself? Gather a group of friends and make signs that explain what you are demonstrating about. Ask an adult to accompany you and stand with your signs in a safe public place. A good idea is to make leaflets with information on, so passers-by can learn about the issue you are protesting. You could wear fancy dress to make your demonstration more eye-catching!

WANGARI MAATHAI

Wangari understood how caring for the environment and caring for people were part of the same cause.

ENVIRONMENTALIST

Wangari wanted to protect the natural environment, and improve the lives of rural women, so she started the Green Belt Movement to get people planting trees.

LIVED:	1 April 1940 – 25 September 2011
BORN IN:	Ihithe Village, Nyeri District (Kenya)
WORKED IN:	Nairobi (Kenya)

29

As a little girl Wangari felt a strong connection to nature. Near her house was a fig tree and a stream, and Wangari's mum would send her to collect firewood and water. In the stream, frogs would lay their eggs, and Wangari thought they looked like beautiful beads.

Most girls in rural Kenya like Wangari did not go to school, as education was not considered important for them, however Wangari was very clever and her parents were persuaded to let her study. At high school she was the best student in her class. In 1960, she won a scholarship to Mount St Scholastica College in Kansas, USA, to study biology, chemistry and German. She returned to Kenya to get her PhD – the first East African woman to receive one.

Wangari saw that people in Kenya were facing many problems. In rural areas, there was no firewood, and no water. Without firewood, people could not cook healthy food. Many people were suffering from malnutrition and also didn't have any work.

Wangari realised that many of the problems were due to deforestation. Trees had been cut down to make space for money-earning crops, such as tea. But this meant there was no firewood. The trees had previously helped the land store water and soil, but without the trees, water quickly ran off, taking the soil with it.

She had the idea to help women plant native trees to renew the health of the land, and provide firewood. This was the start of the Green Belt Movement. In the 1980s the government of Kenya was very repressive. Through the Green Belt Movement Wangari also carried out pro-democracy activism, by registering women to vote and pushing for political reform.

The government attempted to shut down the Green Belt Movement, and Wangari's pro-democracy activities. In 1992, Wangari was arrested and released on bail. But during another clash with the government – this time about pro-democracy campaigners who were being held in prison – Wangari was badly beaten and ended up in a coma.

Despite the government attempting to shut it down, the Green Belt Movement became extremely successful, and since it began in 1977 over 51 million trees have been planted in Kenya, and over 30,000 women have been trained in forestry and other environmental skills. In 2002 Wangari ran for Parliament, and was elected to a position in the Ministry for Environment and Natural Resources. In 2004, she won the Nobel Peace Prize for her environmental and pro-democracy work.

HELP THE ENVIRONMENT LIKE WANGARI

There are lots of ways we can help make our environment healthier and happier. Planting wild flowers can provide a home for animals and insects, as well as helping to protect the soil. Have you got any bare patches of ground at home or at school that could be planted with wild flowers? Ask your teacher if you can make a project of planting flowers or even a tree – you will be helping nature thrive, and making your environment a nicer place to be.

MALALA YOUSAFZAI

The youngest ever winner of a Nobel Peace Prize, Malala was just a schoolgirl herself when she was shot for standing up for the rights of girls to have an education.

EDUCATION CAMPAIGNER

Malala set up the Malala Fund, which is an organisation working to ensure every girl in the world receives a minimum of 12 years of education.

BORN:	12 July 1997
BORN IN:	Mingora (Pakistan)
WORKS IN:	Pakistan, the UK and worldwide

Malala was born in an area of Pakistan called the Swat Valley, in a town called Mingora. Her dad was a social activist who campaigned for human rights, and for the right of every child to go to school. He founded many schools in the Swat Valley. Malala understood from a very young age that the situation in the area where her family lived was not fair. The area was controlled by the Taliban, who are a political group that follow a very extreme and repressive version of Islam.

The Taliban use violence to enforce their rules, such as forbidding girls to be educated, banning music, films and television, and even banning women from leaving the house without a male relative. This is very different to the way most Muslims around the world, such as Malala and her family, practice their religion. The Taliban blew up nearly 400 schools, and many of the students in the schools set up by Malala's dad stopped attending due to the danger.

Aged 11, Malala began writing a blog on the BBC website, arguing for her right to continue attending school. She also spoke on a TV talk show, asking 'How dare the Taliban take away my right to a basic education?' When the blog was translated into English, many people around the world read it, and she became very well known. Malala gave more television interviews, and the famous activist and religious leader Desmond Tutu nominated her for the International Children's Peace Prize.

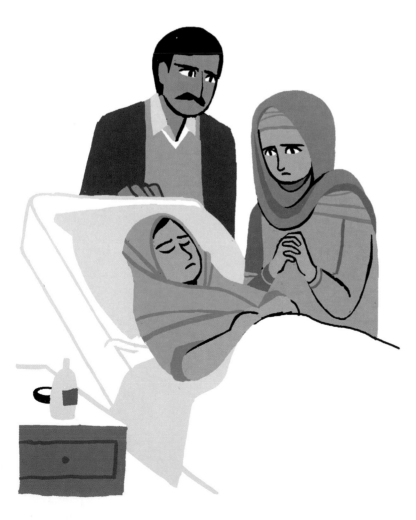

Then, when Malala was 15, a Taliban gunman boarded the bus that was taking her home from school and shot her in the head, in an attempt to kill her. Malala was very ill, but the bullet did not reach her brain. She was flown to hospital a few hours away, and then transferred to a hospital in England. She slowly recovered, and began going to school in Birmingham, England, where her family now also live.

A year later she gave a speech at the United Nations about her experiences and the right of all girls to get an education. In 2014, when she was only 17, she became the youngest ever recipient of the Nobel Peace Prize for her activism. She continues to mix campaigning for girls' rights to education with her own studies. She has called on world leaders to invest in 'books, not bullets'.

HELP EVERY CHILD LEARN LIKE MALALA

You might think that you aren't yet old enough to be a teacher. Wrong! No matter what your age is, you can help another young person learn. Get your friends involved too. Start a buddy scheme and pair up your friends with younger students in your school. You can then all meet up with your younger buddies for short reading sessions. Get the younger students to read aloud to their older buddy. The older students can help their younger buddies with any difficult words, and help them learn to read aloud.

MORE SOCIAL ACTIVISM HEROES

There are a great many other inspiring women who are social activists and leaders. Here are even more courageous and tireless campaigners for justice, from the past right up to the present day.

KATE SHEPPARD

LIVED: 10 March 1847 – 13 July 1934

BORN IN: Liverpool (UK)

WORKED IN: New Zealand

Kate grew up and went to school in Scotland, and from an early age she had a reputation for being very clever. She moved to New Zealand with her mum and siblings in 1868, where she began to get involved in various causes. She believed that women should be able to participate in all aspects of society, including politics, at a time when women did not have the vote anywhere in the world. Kate was a strong believer in equality of all kinds, saying, 'all that separates, whether of race, class, creed, or sex, is inhuman, and must be overcome.'

She wrote many pamphlets, and held meetings in favour of women's suffrage (the right to vote). During the late 1880s and 1890s Kate organised several petitions on women's suffrage which were presented to Parliament. Finally, in 1893, she presented the largest petition yet and that year a bill was passed granting women in New Zealand the vote – the first country in the world to do so. She continued to campaign for women's rights for several years until she was prevented by ill health. She is now considered a very important figure in New Zealand's history, and the history of women's suffrage worldwide. Kate's portrait is printed on the New Zealand ten dollar note.

QIU JIN

LIVED: 8 November 1875 – 15 July 1907

BORN IN: Shaoxing (China)

WORKED IN: China

Hands off our feet!

Qiu Jin was born to a reasonably well-off family in China. She had an arranged marriage to a man named Wang Tingjun, but their relationship was not a happy one, as her husband had no time for Qiu Jin's feminist ideas. In 1904 she left her husband and two children to study in Japan, where she set up a feminist group calling for women's rights, particularly freedom to marry who they wish, freedom of education, and an end to the tradtition of foot-binding, which she herself had suffered. Foot-binding was a traditional Chinese custom where the bones in a girl's feet were deliberately broken, and the toes curled under the feet and tightly bound to make the foot smaller. Small feet were seen to be beautiful. It was very painful and often resulted in infection and disability. Qiu Jin planned with some other revolutionaries to overthrow the Chinese ruling regime. However, her plans were discovered and she was beheaded. She is now a symbol of women's independence in China.

ELEANOR ROOSEVELT

LIVED: 11 October 1884 – 7 November 1962
BORN IN: New York City, New York (USA)
WORKED IN: USA

Eleanor's parents both died before she was 11. She went to school in England, and then returned to the USA, where she married Franklin Roosevelt. Franklin became President of the United States in 1933, making Eleanor 'First Lady'. Previously it had been the role of First Ladies to host parties and entertain guests, but Eleanor was determined to make a difference. She spoke out on behalf of women, children and black people, giving regular press conferences and writing a newspaper column. After Franklin Roosevelt died in 1945, Eleanor became a delegate to the United Nations, where she helped draft the Universal Declaration of Human Rights.

ROSA PARKS

LIVED: 4 February 1913 – 24 October 2005
BORN IN: Tuskegee, Alabama (USA)
WORKED IN: USA

Get up!

No!

In Alabama where Rosa lived, there was a set of laws called 'segregation' that kept black people and white people separate. Black people had to go to different schools to white people, and on buses, they had separate seating areas. If all the seats were full, black passengers had to give up their seats for white passengers. On 1 December 1955, Rosa was arrested when she refused to give up her seat to a white passenger. In response to her arrest, black people in the city of Montgomery boycotted (refused to use) the buses for over a year. The bus companies lost a lot of money, and eventually the law concerning the buses was changed. However, it wasn't until 1964 that segregation of public spaces was abolished across the USA.

MAYA ANGELOU

LIVED: 4 April 1928 – 28 May 2014
BORN IN: St Louis, Missouri (USA)
WORKED IN: USA

Maya's real name was 'Marguerite', but when she was little her brother would call her 'My-a sister', and the nickname 'Maya' stuck. It wasn't an easy childhood, as the society in southern USA where she lived was very racist. When she was eight, she was abused by her mum's boyfriend. She told her mum about it, and when her mum's boyfriend was later found murdered, Maya believed her voice had killed him. She didn't speak for five years after that. When she grew up, she had many jobs, working as a waitress, a singer, an actor and a dancer. She joined the civil rights movement, campaigning alongside well-known activists such as Malcolm X and Martin Luther King. But her true passion was always for writing. In 1969 she wrote the story of her life, *I Know Why the Caged Bird Sings*. It became a bestseller, and helped many people to understand what life was like for a black woman growing up in a racist society.

ELLEN JOHNSON SIRLEAF

BORN: 29 October 1938
BORN IN: Monrovia (Liberia)
WORKS IN: Liberia

Ellen is from Liberia, a country with a troubled history. Liberia was settled as a colony for freed black and mixed-heritage slaves from the USA in the early 19th century. However, the area of land already had people living there, and a very oppressive class-system was put in place, with immigrants holding power over the indigenous African people. Ellen had a mixture of immigrant and indigenous heritage, and she did very well in school. As an adult she began working in government.

In 1980, the President and many ministers were shot during a military coup. The leader of the coup, Samuel Doe, declared himself president, and later he put Ellen in prison for criticising him. In 1989 Samuel Doe was overthrown by another man, Charles Taylor, and Liberia was plunged into a violent civil war, which killed over a quarter of a million people.

After 13 years of fighting, Charles Taylor agreed to leave Liberia, and in 2005 Ellen was elected the president, the first woman president of any African country. She made education free and compulsory for all children. In 2011, alongside Nigerian peace activist Leymah Gbowee, Ellen won the Nobel Peace Prize, for their work in bringing in a period of peace and stability in Liberia.

I swear to clean up the mess you men have made.

EUFROSINA CRUZ

BORN: 1 January 1979

BORN IN: Santa Maria Quiegolani, Oaxaca (Mexico)

WORKS IN: Mexico

Eufrosina comes from an indigenous community in Mexico, where traditional laws and ways of life mean that most women have to get up very early to gather fuel, grind corn to make tortillas and look after the children. Girls have little education, and their husbands are often chosen for them by their fathers. Aged 11, Eufrosina decided she wanted a better life than this. She saved up money by selling chewing gum, and went away to study. When she returned, she was determined to make women's lives better in her community, so she became a candidate in the election for mayor. She won many votes, but the men who ran the community were furious, and cancelled the election result, saying she could not be mayor because she was a woman. Eufrosina wrote to the Human Rights Commission, and got the local laws changed so that women could participate fully in elections. She also started an organisation, QUIEGO, to achieve justice for indigenous women.

MANAL AL-SHARIF

BORN: 25 April 1979

BORN IN: Mecca (Saudi Arabia)

WORKS IN: Saudi Arabia

In Saudi Arabia the laws governing what women are allowed to do are very restrictive. Women have not been allowed to drive cars, or travel without a male relative's permission. After spending some time in the USA where she could drive freely, Manal returned to Saudi Arabia, and she decided enough was enough. She borrowed her brother's car, and filmed herself driving, and put the video on YouTube. The video was watched 700,000 times in a single day. She started receiving death threats, and was arrested and put in prison for a week, but her act inspired other women to do the same. On 17 June 2011 over a hundred women got into their cars and drove, while police watched. Finally, in 2017 the law was changed so that women are allowed to drive.

AMELIA TELFORD

BORN: 1994

BORN IN: Tweed Heads (Australia)

WORKS IN: Australia

Bundjalung country, where Amelia Telford is from, is a part of Australia with a beautiful and diverse landscape. There are beaches, rainforest and mountains, and it is an area where many indigenous Australian people live. Amelia loved the natural landscape of her home, but gradually realised how climate change was impacting both the environment, and the indigenous people who lived in the area. So she started working with the Australian Youth Climate Coalition to raise money to create the Seed Indigenous Youth Climate Network, an organisation dedicated to helping young indigenous people take action against climate change.

GET INVOLVED IN SOCIAL ACTIVISM!

There are lots of different ways to be an activist. Activists stand up for what they believe in. Activists let other people know about the unfair things that are happening around the world. Activists use their own special talents and gifts to get their words heard. Activists raise money for organisations that are challenging injustice. Activists see what needs to be done, and they don't give up. Here are some ideas for how you can get involved in social activism.

MAKE AN ONLINE VIDEO

Unless people know about an issue, they can't do anything about it! So raising awareness is a very important part of social activism. There are many different ways of spreading your message, but one great way is through online videos. These can be shared over and over again. Lots of charities and organisations use videos to get their messages across, so try watching some of them online for inspiration. While you watch, think about what makes their videos especially powerful or moving, and then try creating your own. Make sure you check with your parents before putting videos of yourself online.

START A PETITION

It can be difficult to convince the people in charge that things need to change. That's when you need to prove that you are not alone. You need to show that there are a lot of people on your side who also want things to be done differently. This is what a petition is for! A petition is a list of names of people who agree with you about what needs to be done, and the more people you can get to sign it, the louder your collective voice is. You can start petitions online or, if your issue is something close to home – perhaps you want to petition your school to compost the canteen food waste, or put up some nesting boxes for birds – you can simply collect names and signatures on sheets of paper and hand-deliver them to the person in charge.

RAISE MONEY FOR CHARITY

Effective action on big issues can take a lot of time and money, which is why non-governmental organisations (NGOs) and charities are needed to work in a long-term, and organised way. Raising money for an organisation of your choice can be a fun way to help support the causes you care about. There are tons of ways to raise money: you could do a sponsored walk or bike ride. You could collect up your old toys and clothes and hold a jumble sale. You could organise a party, or get your friends together to put on a musical performance and charge people for tickets. Be creative!

LEARN TO WIN AN ARGUMENT

Making change happen often requires a lot of people to be convinced of something that they disagree with, or maybe aren't sure about. Learning how to make a convincing argument for your point of view is a really useful skill, not only in social activism but in other areas of life too! One way to get better at arguing your case is through debating. Search for debate clubs in your local area, or read up about the rules of formal debating online. In debate clubs you often have to argue the case for something you don't actually agree with, which is a great way to sharpen your skills, as well as helping you understand other people's points of view.

GLOSSARY

Abolitionist movement A campaign in Europe and the USA in the 18th and 19th centuries to make slavery illegal.

Aboriginal people Indigenous people from mainland Australia.

Advocate Someone who argues on behalf of another person or group of people.

American Civil War A war fought in the USA from 1861 to 1865 between southern and northern states over issues such as the right to own slaves.

Census An official survey of the population of a country to find out how many people live there and to collect other information about them.

Democracy A system of government in which all the people of a country can vote to elect their representatives.

Feminism A belief that women should have the same rights as men.

Genus A category of something.

Governess A woman who was employed to look after and teach children in a private house.

Great Depression An economic event that occurred across many countries in the 1930s where businesses went bankrupt and many people were unemployed.

Ideology A set of political beliefs and ideas.

Indigenous people Descendants of people who have always lived in a particular area, as opposed to later immigrants and their descendants.

Islam The religion of Muslims.

League of Nations An organisation set up after the First World War to try and promote world peace through international negotiation.

Malnutrition Poor health caused by not having enough food or a healthy diet.

Morality The belief that some behaviour is right and acceptable and that other behaviour is wrong.

Nazi A member of the right-wing political party, led by Adolf Hitler, which was in power in Germany from 1933 to 1945.

Oppression Cruel or unjust treatment.

Pacifism The belief that violence is never justified.

Pamphlet A short book or leaflet containing arguments about a particular subject.

Philosophy The study of the nature and meaning of human life and of the universe.

Preacher A person who gives religious speeches.

Referendum A vote to decide a specific political question.

Seamstress A woman who makes a living from sewing.

Segregation A historical set of laws in the USA ruling that black and white people had to use different services and facilities such as schools or drinking fountains.

Suffrage The right to vote.

Treason The crime of betraying your country.

United Nations An international organisation formed in 1945 to try and improve human rights around the world and maintain peace.

FURTHER INFORMATION

WEBSITES

The BBC Children in Need, Save the Children and Unicef websites have lots of ideas for how to raise money for important causes.
bbcchildreninneed.co.uk/fundraisinghub
www.savethechildren.org.uk/how-you-can-help/events-and-fundraising
www.unicef.org.uk/fundraise/fundraise-in-your-community/at-school

Change.org is a website that allows you to set up and share a petition online.
www.change.org

Contact your local MP or politician to let them know about a problem affecting people in your local area or to ask for their support on a particular campaign that you feel strongly about.
www.parliament.uk/get-involved/contact-your-mp

BOOKS

Rebel Voices: The Rise of Votes for Women by Louise Kay Stewart and Eve Lloyd Knight (Wren and Rook, 2018)

This Book Will Help You Change the World by Sue Turton and Alice Skinner (Wren and Rook, 2017)

Suffragettes and the Fight for the Vote by Sarah Ridley (Franklin Watts, 2017)

Fantastically Great Women Who Changed the World by Kate Pankhurst (Bloomsbury, 2016)

I am Malala (young readers edition) by Malala Yousafzai and Patricia McCormick (Orion Children's Books, 2014)

INDEX

First published in Great Britain in 2018 by Wayland
Copyright © Hodder and Stoughton, 2018

All rights reserved.

Editor: Sarah Silver
Designer: Lisa Peacock

Wayland, an imprint of Hachette Children's Group
Part of Hodder & Stoughton
Carmelite House
50 Victoria Embankment
London EC4Y 0DZ

ISBN: 978 1 5263 0471 1

10 9 8 7 6 5 4 3 2 1

Printed and bound in China

An Hachette UK Company
www.hachette.co.uk
www.hachettechildrens.co.uk

MIX
Paper from responsible sources
FSC® C104740
FSC www.fsc.org

DISCOVER MORE ...

BRILLIANT WOMEN

AMAZING ARTISTS AND DESIGNERS

Artemisia Gentileschi
Rosa Bonheur
Edmonia Lewis
Coco Chanel
Frida Kahlo
Yayoi Kusama
Vivienne Westwood
Zaha Hadid
Judith Leyster
Harriet Powers
Georgia O'Keeffe
Barbara Hepworth
Lee Millar
Emily Kame Kngwarreye
Louise Bourgeois
Bastardilla
Kara Walker

HEROIC LEADERS AND ACTIVISTS

Mary Wollstonecraft
Harriet Tubman
Eglantyne Jebb
Helen Keller
Faith Bandler
Sophie Scholl
Wangari Maathai
Malala Yousafzai
Kate Sheppard
Qiu Jin
Eleanor Roosevelt
Rosa Parks
Maya Angelou
Ellen Johnson Sirleaf
Eufrosina Cruz
Manal Al-Sharif
Amelia Telford

INCREDIBLE SPORTING CHAMPIONS

Marie Marvingt
Babe Didrikson Zaharias
Cathy Freeman
Sarah Storey
Serena Williams
Marta
Tatyana McFadden
Ellie Simmonds
Yuenü
Lis Hartel
Billie Jean King
Patti McGee
Kaori Icho
Nicola Adams
Tirunesh Dibaba
Ibtihaj Muhammad
Simone Biles

PIONEERS OF SCIENCE AND TECHNOLOGY

Caroline Herschel
Mary Anning
Ada Lovelace
Marie Curie
Lise Meitner
Barbara McClintock
Katherine Johnson
Jane Goodall
Hypatia
Mary Somerville
Rachel Carson
Dorothy Hodgkin
Chien-Shiung Wu
Rosalind Franklin
Indira Nath
Wanda Díaz Merced
Juliana Rotich

WAYLAND
www.waylandbooks.co.uk